Matthias and the Miracle Meal

A Christian Tale

Retold and illustrated by Andy Robb

Hachette UK's policy is to use papers that are natural, renewable and recyclable products and made from wood grown in well-managed forests and other controlled sources. The logging and manufacturing processes are expected to conform to the environmental regulations of the country of origin.

ISBN: 9781398377257

Text © Andy Robb
Design, illustrations and layout © 2023 Hodder & Stoughton Limited
First published in 2023 by Hodder & Stoughton Limited (for its Hodder Education imprint, part of the Hodder Education Group),
An Hachette UK Company
Carmelite House, 50 Victoria Embankment, London EC4Y 0DZ
www.hoddereducation.com

Impression number 10 9 8 7 6 5 4 3 2 1
Year 2027 2026 2025 2024 2023

Author and illustrator: Andy Robb
Series Editor: Catherine Coe
Commissioning Editor: Hamish Baxter
Educational Reviewer: Pauline Allen
Design and page layouts: Helen Townson
Editors: Amy Tyrer, Gaelle Lefevre

With thanks to Walk Through the Bible for expert information and advice.

With thanks to the schools that took part in the development of *Reading Planet* KS2, including: Ancaster CE Primary School, Ancaster; Downsway Primary School, Reading; Ferry Lane Primary School, London; Foxborough Primary School, Slough; Griffin Park Primary School, Blackburn; St Barnabas CE First & Middle School, Pershore; Tranmoor Primary School, Doncaster; and Wilton CE Primary School, Wilton.

The publishers would like to thank the following for permission to reproduce copyright material.
Cover and internals © Marina Zlochin/stock.adobe.com; p38 © Renáta Sedmáková/stock.adobe.com; p39 © Natis/stock.adobe.com; p39 © Jeremetok/stock.adobe.com

All rights reserved. Apart from any use permitted under UK copyright law, no part of this publication may be reproduced or transmitted in any form or by any means, electronic or mechanical, including photocopying and recording, or held within any information storage and retrieval system, without permission in writing from the publisher or under licence from the Copyright Licensing Agency Limited. Further details of such licences (for reprographic reproduction) may be obtained from the Copyright Licensing Agency Limited, https://www.cla.co.uk/

A catalogue record for this title is available from the British Library.

Printed in India.

Orders: Please contact Hachette UK Distribution, Hely Hutchinson Centre, Milton Road, Didcot, Oxfordshire, OX11 7HH. Telephone: +44 (0)1235 400555. Lines are open from 9 a.m. to 5 p.m., Monday to Friday. Email: primary@hachette.co.uk

Contents

Chapter 1 4

Chapter 2 11

Chapter 3 18

Chapter 4 24

Chapter 5 33

What Is Christianity? 38

Chapter 1

You may think it odd when I tell you that we are going to begin this Christian tale in the land of Israel, home to the Jewish people. What on earth have Christianity and the Jews got to do with each other? Well, you're about to meet a young Jewish lad called Matthias and, as we follow his story, everything will become clear.

Matthias lived in Israel around 2000 years ago, when it was part of the vast Roman Empire. This stretched from Spain in the west to Mesopotamia in the east. The Romans had been in charge for the whole of Matthias's life.

Being Jewish meant that Matthias didn't worship the gods of the Romans, but the one God of the Jewish people. Most of the time this wasn't a problem. The Romans generally let the Jews carry on with their customs as long as they didn't cause trouble and they paid their taxes to the emperor.

But trouble was coming.

One morning, Matthias was busy spying on the Romans. The day was already hot, so Matthias had taken shelter under the shade of an olive tree at the edge of the village. High up in the olive grove was his favourite spying spot. Here, Matthias had a clear view of the road that wound down from the surrounding hills and into the village below.

But it wasn't Roman soldiers that Matthias was looking out for. They were everywhere and you could see them a mile off in their striking red uniforms. It was Roman spies that Matthias was interested in. They tried to blend in by disguising themselves as locals or travelling merchants. Their job was to look out for Jewish people who might be plotting against the Roman rulers and to report back their findings.

Matthias prided himself on being able to identify the Roman spies despite their attempts to hide. He secretly admired them because of their skill and courage, but that didn't stop Matthias wanting to become a spy for his own people. Maybe he could collect enough undercover information to help the Jews rise up against the Romans and finally send them packing. They were fed up being told what to do by the Romans. The Jews just wanted Israel back to themselves.

One thing Matthias had learned about spying was that it was important to keep a note of what you observe. For this, he used a writing tablet, which he carried about with him almost everywhere. He was meant to use it at school but Matthias much preferred spying to studying.

His dad often said, "Matthias, if you spent as much time studying as you do spying on the Romans, you would be top of your class and make your mother and me proud."

It wasn't that Matthias didn't want to learn about the Jewish scriptures, such as the Torah or the Prophets. It was just that he couldn't see what use they would be to him if he wanted to be a spy one day.

Matthias's patience was finally rewarded. In the distance, he spotted someone coming down the road. Matthias was certain the man was a Roman spy. With his writing tablet at the ready, Matthias began to make notes of what he saw.

Matthias had devised a way of jotting things down using pictures and as few words as possible. It not only saved time when he was on one of his missions, it also stopped other people from knowing what he had discovered. It was his very own code and only he knew how to decipher it.

Matthias squinted in the bright sunlight, trying to see what else he could find out about the Roman spy, when a girl's voice pierced the stillness of the day.

"There you are, Matthias. I've been looking for you everywhere." It was his little sister, Abigail. Her timing couldn't have been worse. The Roman spy was alerted by Abigail's shrill voice and glanced up towards where Matthias was hiding. The spy gave him a friendly wave. How embarrassing! Not only had Matthias been spotted, but the Roman spy obviously didn't think that an eight-year-old boy was anything to worry about.

Matthias got to his feet grouchily and went to find out what his sister wanted. It was pointless pretending he hadn't been seen – his cover had been blown. In future, he'd have to find another place from which to do his spying.

"What do you want, Abigail?" Matthias snapped. "Couldn't you see that I was on a top-secret mission for our nation?"

Ignoring her brother's grumbling, Abigail continued, "Sorry, Matthias, but there's no time for that. Mum said you've got to come home right away."

"What's the hurry?" Matthias asked. "Can't our midday meal wait a few minutes?"

"It's not that, Matthias," explained Abigail. "Apparently, Jesus is crossing the Sea of Galilee and heading our way. The whole village is going out to see him. Mum and Dad told me to fetch you and to come quick. We're going to see him too."

Chapter 2

By the time Matthias and Abigail got back home, the village was almost deserted. Normally the place was bustling with people going about their daily business, but not now. The only people left behind were those too old or infirm to go chasing after Jesus.

"There you are!" said his dad. "Another day I'll talk to you about the amount of time you fritter away playing spies, Matthias. Right now, we need to get a move on if we're to be in with a chance of seeing Jesus. Most of the village left a good fifteen minutes ago. If we want to catch up with them, we need to get going now."

Dad handed Matthias his leather bag, which he took almost everywhere with him.

"You'll need to take this, Matthias," Dad said, "so that I can carry your sister some of the way. The terrain is hilly and her little legs will slow us down."

Still holding on to his writing tablet with one hand, Matthias took the bag from his dad with the other and flung it over his shoulder. His body flinched under the weight.

What on earth was in the bag? But Matthias didn't have time to undo the leather straps and take a sneaky peek inside. His family were already striding up the hill that led out of the village and into the open countryside. Matthias put his curiosity to one side and raced after them.

At the top of the hill, they could see for miles in every direction. In the distance, Matthias caught sight of a large group of people heading towards the Sea of Galilee.

"There they are!" Matthias announced at the top of his voice. "It won't take long for us to catch up with them."

Now that they could see the other villagers, Matthias breathed a sigh of relief.

He'd heard so much about Jesus, and missing out on this opportunity to see him would have been a huge disappointment.

As they carried on walking, questions popped into Matthias's head. That wasn't unusual. Matthias always had questions, such as:

"Dad, why is the sky blue?"

"Mum, why do I have to eat my vegetables?"

"Dad, why did God make wasps?"

And so it went on.

Today, Matthias's questions were about Jesus.

"Dad, is this Jesus the Messiah that we're taught about at school?"

"To be honest, Matthias, I don't know," his dad replied. "Our teachings say that when the Messiah comes he will be like the Prophet Moses, who performed mighty miracles back when our people were slaves in Egypt."

Miracles! That was a big clue for Matthias. He'd heard that Jesus was performing miracles. He needed to write this down. Matthias stopped walking for a moment and scribbled some notes on his writing tablet. Investigating Roman spies could wait. Investigating Jesus was his new mission now.

Matthias ran to catch up with his family. He had another question. "Dad, we're also taught that the Messiah will be a great teacher. Isn't that what Jesus is?"

"You're right, my boy. He is," his dad said, smiling. "I've heard that when Jesus talks about God, it's as if God himself were speaking to you. But they say he also speaks in ways that ordinary people like us can understand. Our religious leaders have never done that. It's why they're so jealous of him."

Matthias scribbled down the information his dad had just given him as he kept walking.

He launched into yet another question before his dad changed the subject. "Doesn't Jesus say that we are to love our enemies?"

"That's right, Matthias, he does," his dad agreed. "But a lot of us were hoping that God would send someone to set us free from the Romans. It doesn't sound like Jesus has plans to do anything like that."

'Love your enemies' Matthias wrote on his tablet, but in code, of course.

That was enough questions for now, thought Matthias. His head was almost full to bursting as he tried to work out whether or not Jesus was the Messiah that his people had been waiting for. He was also finding it hard to concentrate because of his excitement about actually seeing Jesus in person very soon.

Chapter 3

Walking quickly, it didn't take long for Matthias and his family to catch up with the rest of the village. There were lots of faces he recognised. Friends from school, neighbours, shopkeepers. There were plenty of people that he didn't know too. The news about Jesus had obviously reached towns and villages right across the region.

There were family groups just like theirs, as well as couples, people on their own and even animals adding to the noise and excitement.

And then Matthias felt something rub against his leg and heard, "Meow."

"Those stray cats get everywhere," he muttered to himself.

The cat rubbed itself up against Matthias's leg for a second time.

"Will you go away, you silly cat?" he said, striding forwards.

"Meow," it said again.

Matthias looked down to give the annoying cat its final warning but then changed his mind. "I'm going to call you Tiberius," said Matthias. "With your strange, staring eyes and scowling mouth you look just like that rotten Roman emperor Tiberius, who has been making our lives such a misery."

Tiberius looked up and meowed at Matthias again.

As Matthias and his family continued walking, the cat followed close behind.

By the middle of the afternoon, Matthias finally caught a glimpse of what they had all been looking for. There, in the valley below, was the Sea of Galilee, glistening in the sun. Matthias could see that the people at the front of the crowd were already on the shore.

He could also just about make out a couple of empty fishing boats drawn up onto the stony beach. But Jesus was nowhere to be seen.

Then Matthias saw the people on the shore looking up into the nearby hills. Suddenly, there was much pointing and shouting. Matthias couldn't hear what they were saying but it was obvious that someone had spotted Jesus. He looked in the direction they were pointing and scanned the hillside.

And then he saw him. A few hundred feet up the side of the small mountain sat a group of men. It was Jesus and his disciples. These were the twelve men Jesus had handpicked to accompany him as he travelled around doing miracles and teaching people about God.

Matthias had heard about the disciples. These men were from all walks of life, including fishermen and a tax collector who'd actually worked for the hated Romans. Jesus didn't seem to be fussy about who he hung out with. He loved everybody.

The people on the shore began clambering up the rocky slope to where Jesus and his disciples were sitting. Those on higher ground, like Matthias and his family, continued across the mountain towards Jesus.

Matthias was amazed by the size of the crowd swarming towards Jesus. Thousands and thousands of people were coming from just about every direction, all eager to see him. In Jewish culture, it was normal only to count the men, and Matthias guessed there must have been around 5000 of them. But what if you added the women and children to that? Who knew how many there were – 10,000? 15,000? 20,000?

The crowd was so big that it was now moving at a much slower pace. Matthias used this as an opportunity to stop and make more notes.

For fun, Matthias also drew a picture of Tiberius. He couldn't leave him out. For some reason the cat wouldn't stop following him.

In all of the excitement, Matthias had completely forgotten that he had missed out on his midday meal. Until now. His tummy quietly rumbled under his tunic to remind him.

Why had his mum and dad been in such a rush, Matthias thought grumpily? They could have at least grabbed something to eat before setting out. Surely a few extra minutes wouldn't have made much of a difference. There weren't even any nearby villages where they could buy food.

It was all just rugged hillsides and open country for as far as the eye could see.

Chapter 4

"Meow."

Once again, Matthias could feel soft fur rubbing against his leg. It was Tiberius, now trying to look cute and friendly. The stray cat meowed again, and Matthias guessed that he was hungry.

Matthias shrugged and apologised, "Sorry, Tiberius, I can't help you there. I'm as hungry as you are."

Tiberius didn't seem deterred. He shifted his gaze to the leather bag slung over Matthias's shoulder and purred again.

At that moment the crowd ground to an abrupt halt. Those at the front had finally reached Jesus and the effect of them stopping rippled back through the crowd, bringing everyone else to a standstill. Matthias tried to peer over the sea of people now blocking his view. He couldn't believe that they had come this far only to be stuck at the back of the crowd. What a letdown!

He pulled a disappointed face at his dad.

"Sorry, Matthias," Dad said. "It was worth a try. I knew Jesus was popular but I hadn't imagined there would be crowds like this. Why don't we rest our legs and have a bite to eat?"

"A bite to eat?" echoed Matthias. "But we're in the middle of nowhere! Where are we going to find food out here?"

His dad laughed. "In the bag you're carrying. While Abigail was fetching you from the olive grove, I packed up our midday meal into the bag. We've got bread and we've got fish. That should fill a hole."

"Of course! That's why this cat has been following us," said Matthias. "He could smell the fish!"

Tiberius purred knowingly.

Matthias looked around him, and at Jesus far off in the distance. Hang on a minute, he thought. Had he come all this way just to have a picnic? No! His mission had been to meet Jesus. His rumbling tummy could wait. There was no way he was going to miss this chance.

"Wait, there's something I have to do before we eat," Matthias said. "I'll be back very soon." And with that, Matthias shot off into the crowd, still carrying his dad's leather bag over his shoulder.

Being eight years old had its advantages. Matthias was able to weave his way through the crowd with ease – under legs and around them. He had always been light on his feet and in no time at all he found himself nearing the front of the crowd. Just one last spurt and he'd be there.

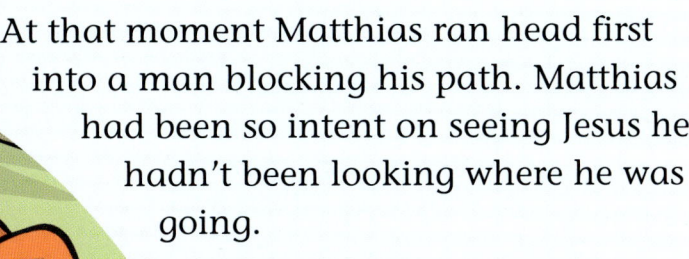

At that moment Matthias ran head first into a man blocking his path. Matthias had been so intent on seeing Jesus he hadn't been looking where he was going.

"Whoa! Not so fast, lad," the man chuckled. "You'll be over the edge of the mountain if you aren't careful."

Matthias looked up to see a burly man with a bushy, brown beard standing over him. Being an observant spy, Matthias recognised him as one of the men he'd seen on the mountainside with Jesus.

For once, Matthias was at a loss for words. He couldn't believe that he was actually talking to one of Jesus's disciples. He also couldn't believe that he'd ruined everything by almost knocking the man over.

27

But the man put out his hand and hauled Matthias to his feet. "No harm done," he said.

As Matthias brushed the dust off of his clothes, the man sniffed … and then sniffed again.

"If I'm not very much mistaken, I smell fish," he said.

"You're right," said Matthias, pointing to his bag. "My dad packed it for our lunch. There's bread as well."

The man had a question for Matthias. "Would you mind sharing your food with everyone? Say no if you'd rather not."

Matthias thought for a moment. The first thing that came to his mind was to wonder how his food could possibly feed so many people. But the next thing that popped into his head was something his dad had said to him about Jesus.

Matthias's mind was made up. He opened the leather bag and handed its contents to the man. There were five loaves and two fish. He was sure his dad wouldn't mind.

"Yes, of course you can have them. But I'm not sure there's enough to go round …"

"We'll see!" said the man as he turned and took the loaves and fish to Jesus.

Matthias could see that Jesus was pleased when the man handed him the loaves and fish but he couldn't make out what the two of them were saying – they were too far off.

The man pointed over to Matthias and he realised that they were talking about him. Jesus looked across at Matthias, smiled and mouthed, "Thank you," to him.

Wow! Matthias couldn't believe it. But there were more surprises to come.

Jesus gathered his disciples around him and appeared to give them instructions.

What was Jesus up to? Matthias didn't have to wait long to find out. The men disappeared into the vast crowd and began to ask people to sit down on the grass.

Now that everyone was sitting down, Matthias could see across the crowd to where his mum, dad and sister were. He gave them a quick wave to let them know that he was okay.

Jesus took the loaves and the fish and gave thanks to God for them. He began breaking the loaves and fish into pieces and gave some to each of his disciples. They headed back into the waiting crowd.

The disciples handed out bread and fish to the people and Matthias noticed something strange happening. It was as if their hands kept getting topped up with more and more food. It wasn't only the disciples who seemed to have more than enough. Everyone they gave food to ended up with lots in their hands. Matthias had totally forgotten about taking notes – he was too absorbed with what was happening before his eyes.

Even so, his tummy hadn't forgotten that it was hungry. With a loud rumble, it reminded Matthias that he also needed some of the bread and fish. The disciple Matthias had bumped into earlier was the one who brought him his share of the food.

"Here, have some of your food, young man. By the way, my name's Andrew. I'm one of Jesus's close friends."

"I know," said Matthias. "I've seen you with him. And my name's Matthias."

"Well, thank you, Matthias," said Andrew. "Without you, this miracle meal wouldn't have been possible."

Chapter 5

Not only was everyone now full of food, but Matthias noticed the baskets of leftovers that the disciples were going around collecting. There seemed to be more leftovers than there had been food to begin with. Andrew was right. It had been a miracle meal. Although he'd played his part, Matthias knew that the miracle was all down to Jesus.

Matthias thought he should go back to his family now, but before he did so he needed to make a note of what he'd seen.

As Matthias picked his way through the people, he caught sight of a familiar face. He was sure it was the Roman spy he'd seen earlier in the day. He was no longer wearing his disguise but it was definitely still him.

Matthias noticed that he was talking to Jesus and the disciples. They were hugging and smiling as if they were long-lost friends.

Had the Roman spy swapped sides and become a follower of Jesus? It certainly looked that way. As if to confirm Matthias's suspicions, the man suddenly caught sight of Matthias and gave him an even bigger wave than before.

That got Matthias thinking. He glanced down at the notes on his writing tablet. The things he'd seen and heard about Jesus seemed to speak for themselves. His mind was made up. As far as Matthias was concerned, Jesus was the Messiah.

Before, Matthias had been excited about being a spy when he grew up. But becoming a disciple of Jesus, like Andrew and the Roman spy, seemed like an even greater adventure. Maybe he'd have to wait for a few years, but in the meantime Matthias decided he'd use his investigative abilities to learn more about Jesus from now on.

"Where have you been?" said Matthias's mum when he got back. "It's one thing wandering off alone in our small village – at least we know where you are. But wandering off in such a large crowd is a different matter!"

Matthias suddenly felt something familiar rub against his leg. It was Tiberius, the stray cat.

"I've never seen a cat eat so much," said Abigail. "I don't know where he came from, but he's eaten so much fish I'm surprised he doesn't go pop."

Matthias's dad affectionately ruffled his hair. "Did you manage to get some of the food that Jesus's disciples passed around?" his dad asked. "If not, you can eat the food that's in the leather bag before we set off for home."

"I've had plenty to eat, Dad," Matthias replied, "but there's something else I have to tell you." Matthias showed them the empty leather bag. "All the food is gone. It was our loaves and fish that Jesus used to feed everyone! And all because I didn't give up on trying to meet Jesus."

"Well," said his dad, "perhaps there has been some good to come from this investigating of yours after all."

Matthias laughed. "That's the first time you've ever said that, Dad. I'll definitely need to record *that* on my writing tablet."

What Is Christianity?

A Christian story

This story is traditionally known by Christians as 'The feeding of the 5000' and can be found in four books of the Bible. One of these is John, Chapter 6, Verses 1 to 15. It shows how Christianity and the Jewish people are connected. Jesus was a Jew but it wasn't only the Jewish people he came to rescue. Jesus came for everyone. A few years after that miracle meal, followers of Jesus began to be called Christians, and they still are today.

What Is Christianity?

Christianity is based on the life and teachings of Jesus Christ. Christians believe he is the Son of God who was sent to restore our relationship with God. Jesus was born in Israel just over 2000 years ago.

What do Christians believe?

Christians believe there is only one God but who shows himself in three different ways – as Father, Son (Jesus) and Holy Spirit. They also believe that God sent his Son, Jesus, to earth as a man to save us from the results of our sins – bad things we do that separate us from God.

What is the Christian holy book?

The Bible is where Christians find out who God is, what he's like and how he wants us to live. The Old Testament part of the Bible covers everything from the creation of the world up to when Jesus was born. The New Testament part of the Bible picks up from there and covers the story of Jesus's life and the start of Christianity.

Who and where do Christians worship?

Christianity is a monotheistic religion, which means people worship one God. Although Christians can worship God at any time, the Bible teaches that they should also worship together. This is done in church buildings, in homes or in fact anywhere people can gather.

What does this story mean to Christians?

The feeding of the 5000 demonstrates how much God cares for people. It also shows us that Jesus wasn't just a man – he was God.

Now answer the questions …

1. Who was Matthias spying on at the start of the story?

2. 'Matthias had devised a way of jotting things down using pictures and as few words as possible.' Think of another word that could be used instead of 'devised'.

3. What happened when Matthias met the stray cat?

4. 'It was Jesus and his disciples.' What does the word 'disciple' mean?

5. Why did Matthias pull a disappointed face at his dad when they were stuck at the back of the crowd?

6. What did you think would happen when Matthias shared his loaves and fish?

7. Why did Matthias decide to stop investigating Roman spies and investigate Jesus instead?

8. Have you read any other stories about miracles like the one in this book? What happened in them?